SERIES 218

In this book, we look up into
the earth's atmosphere to see where
weather comes from, discover how clouds
are formed and learn about the extreme
side of the elements.

LADYBIRD BOOKS

UK | USA | Canada | Ireland | Australia
India | New Zealand | South Africa
Ladybird Books is part of the Penguin Random House group of companies
whose addresses can be found at global.penguinrandomhouse.com.
www.penguin.co.uk   www.puffin.co.uk   www.ladybird.co.uk

Penguin
Random House
UK

First published 2021
001
Copyright © Ladybird Books Ltd, 2021
Printed in China
The authorized representative in the EEA is Penguin Random House Ireland,
Morrison Chambers, 32 Nassau Street, Dublin D02 YH68
A CIP catalogue record for this book is available from the British Library
ISBN: 978-0-241-41736-2
All correspondence to:
Ladybird Books
Penguin Random House Children's
One Embassy Gardens, 8 Viaduct Gardens
London SW11 7BW

Weather

A Ladybird Book

Written by Libby Walden

Illustrated by Tom Frost

Atmosphere and weather

To understand weather, humans must look beyond the blue skies and grey clouds to the layers of air surrounding the earth, known as the "atmosphere".

Stretching up into space for 62,000 miles (99,780 km), the atmosphere is made up of five layers: the troposphere, stratosphere, mesosphere, thermosphere and exosphere.

The atmospheric layer closest to earth is the troposphere. It extends from the earth's surface into space for 6.2 miles (10 km) and contains the thickest, or "densest", air in the atmosphere. Air density is calculated by measuring the amount of gases, or "air molecules", in the air and determining how closely packed together they are.

The troposphere is where almost all types of weather take place. This is because the air within the troposphere contains more water vapour (the gas created when water dries up, or "evaporates") than the other layers in the atmosphere. This means that clouds and rain can only be created at this level.

The movement of air molecules and changes within the water content of air is chaotic. This means that scientists who study the changes in weather, known as "meteorologists", are only able to make short-term weather predictions – up to ten days in advance. A typical weather pattern over an area for a long period of time is recorded as the area's "climate".

1. Troposphere
2. Stratosphere
3. Mesosphere
4. Thermosphere
5. Exosphere

What is weather?

Knowing what weather to expect helps us decide what to wear and what to do with our days. But what do we mean when we talk about "the weather"?

Weather is the condition of the earth's atmosphere over a particular place at a particular time. For example, if it is wet outside, then the weather in that place, at that time, would be described as "rainy". But weather is temporary. It doesn't rain all day every day. The weather changes and moves on – as air moves within the troposphere, as day turns to night or as the seasons change.

As air moves and flows, the weather experienced in different parts of the world differs greatly. There could be heatwaves in Kampala, Uganda, at the same time as monsoon rains flood the streets of Chennai, India.

Weather is made up of several elements, including air temperature, wind, humidity, cloud thickness and air pressure. Air pressure is caused by molecules in the air pressing down on the earth and, as pressure levels change, it affects what type of weather is experienced on the earth's surface. High air pressure is caused by air flowing down and fanning out when it reaches the ground. This stops clouds forming and creates clear skies. As the air rises, it cools, causing clouds to form and, sometimes, creating storms. This happens when air pressure is low.

Studying weather

Using science, mathematics and some of the world's most powerful computers, meteorologists are the scientists who study the earth's climate system and interpret how changes within the atmosphere can cause changes in the weather.

Meteorology is the science of weather, and there are many different jobs within it. Researchers, for example, study measurements made on the ground or from space to improve our understanding of how the atmosphere works. Developers create new technology to measure weather systems and collect data. Consultants advise companies and governments on how weather might affect businesses and people.

One common use of meteorology can be found in the weather reports, or "forecasts", that appear in apps, online and on television. These reports are created by computer models, which take atmospheric measurements from around the world and use mathematical equations to work out how weather patterns will change. Forecasters then interpret this information to create local weather reports.

Weather forecasts allow people to prepare ahead of time, but it is difficult to accurately predict what will happen. Tiny changes in the atmosphere can create completely different weather patterns over a week. This is why forecasts usually only cover a few days at a time.

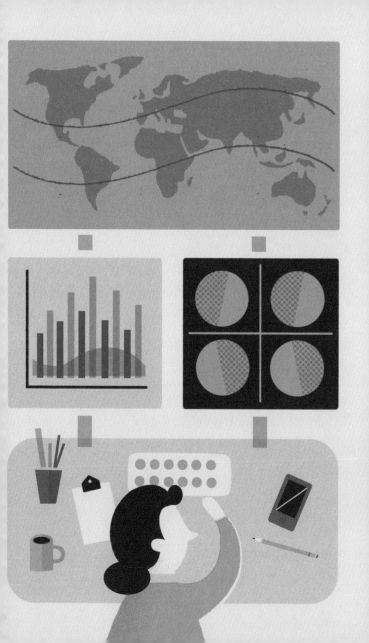

Weather maps

Charts or maps can be used to show the weather conditions in an area at a particular time. Weather maps are created by computers and used by meteorological researchers to plan and predict weather patterns. Early weather maps used simple shapes, such as circles, dots, lines and triangles, to represent each weather event.

Today, when weather forecasts appear in apps, online or as part of the news, weather illustrations are used. They help to show people what weather to expect. The illustrations make it easier and quicker for the public to understand, or "read", the weather map. These maps often include percentages that show how likely it is for a prediction to be true – for example, it might show that there is a 20 per cent chance of rain for that particular day.

Can you tell which weather events are represented on the page opposite? Both the early simple shape and the modern illustration has been included for each one.

1. Rain
2. Hail
3. Snow
4. Wind
5. Sun and clear skies
6. Fog
7. Sunshine with clouds
8. Thunderstorm

Measuring weather

Many different technologies and instruments can be used to "measure" the weather. Here are a few of the simpler instruments that can "read" the weather outside:

- Air pressure can be measured using an instrument called a "barometer". The more widely used "aneroid barometer" looks like a compass and has a metal box inside. Changes in air pressure cause the metal box to swell or shrink. This movement causes the needle on the face of the barometer to turn and show the change in air pressure.

- The direction and speed of wind can be checked by a "windsock". Usually found at airports, windsocks are large material tubes that hang from a pole. In low winds, the windsock will hang loosely. In high winds, it will fly horizontally in the direction the wind is blowing.

- A "thermometer" is used to measure and display the temperature of the air surrounding it. Digital thermometers use a sensor and electrical current to measure changes in air temperature. As the temperature increases, the flow of electricity slows down. By monitoring how easily an electrical current can flow through the sensor, a digital thermometer can interpret the information into a temperature measurement known as a "degree".

24°C

Weather stations

Weather stations are found across the globe, on land and on sea, as well as circling the planet in space as satellites. The sole purpose of a weather station is to collect and log meteorological information all day, every day. Stations collect a huge amount of data, using a variety of instruments to measure the weather outside – everything from wind speed to cloud height.

The position of a weather station is very important. Land-based stations should be situated in an exposed area, with no trees or buildings nearby. This is to make sure that the information they collect is as accurate as possible. Surrounding buildings could reflect heat and create false temperature readings and plants and trees could provide additional shelter and shade, which could affect wind and sunshine measurements.

While ships have long been used to observe weather conditions at sea, weather buoys are now more common, as they can log information on a continuous basis. These floating stations collect information on air temperature and pressure, as well as wave height and speed. The information collected by a weather station is sent via radio, satellite or internet connection to a central computer system and is used, alongside other collected data, to create a larger weather map of the area. Scientists can then use this map for forecasting and research.

Temperature

Air temperature is a measure of how hot or cold the air in the atmosphere is. The temperature of the air on the earth's surface is largely determined by the sun. This giant star at the centre of our solar system produces heat and "electromagnetic radiation" – waves of ultraviolet light.

As these waves travel through the atmosphere, they are filtered and appear as sunshine. The length of time the sun shines and the strength, or "intensity", of the sunshine determines how hot or cold the surface of the earth is. Temperature can be recorded using a thermometer and measured in Celsius or Fahrenheit.

The position of the planet in relation to the sun also affects the air temperature. The earth is a sphere that spins on its axis as it travels around the sun, which means that different parts of the planet are exposed to different intensities of sunshine at different times.

The amount of light and heat that can reach the earth's surface is also dependent on "cloud cover" – the amount of clouds in the sky at any time. Blocked sunlight often means cooler temperatures during the day due to reduced sunlight reaching the earth's surface. But clouds in the sky at night often create a warmer ground temperature, as heat generated by the sun during the day is then trapped within the troposphere.

Extreme heat

High temperatures and lots of sunshine may seem like the perfect weather for a holiday, but extreme heat can be dangerous. When the air temperature rises far above the local average for an extended period of time, it is an extreme weather event called a "heatwave".

Heatwaves are most common during the summer months, when air temperatures are more likely to be high. If an area of land experiences high air pressure for a long period of time, a heatwave can occur. The air flows down and fans out over the ground, making it difficult for clouds to form. Without cloud cover, the sun's light and heat falls directly on to the earth's surface and, over the course of a few days, this can create very high temperatures.

The effects of a heatwave can vary dramatically, but the longer they last and the hotter they become, the more dangerous they are. Intense heatwaves can cause destruction to the natural world and can be dangerous to human health. They can cause crops and plants to wilt and die, wildfires to start in dry areas, and water shortages known as "droughts". To keep safe during a heatwave, humans should drink plenty of water, wear light-coloured, loose clothing and stay out of direct sunlight as much as possible.

Precipitation

When water falls from the sky in any form, it is called "precipitation". Water can fall down to earth in a liquid form, known as "rain", or it can fall in solid forms, known as "hail", "sleet" or "snow".

Precipitation is an important part of what is known as the "water cycle". This chain of events describes the continuous movement of water between the atmosphere, land, ice-covered areas, and oceans. The water cycle has three main stages:

1. Water falls from the sky as rain, sleet, snow or hail. This is precipitation. It falls into bodies of water or on to land, where it runs off into rivers, lakes, streams, seas, areas of groundwater and the ocean.

2. The water is then heated by the sun and is turned into a gas, or "vapour", in a process called "evaporation". The vapour then rises up and enters the troposphere.

3. As the water vapour rises in the troposphere, it cools. Then, as the air cools, water vapour "condenses" back into its liquid form and cloud droplets are created. Over time, these droplets collide and combine to create larger, heavier droplets that then fall back down to earth. This completes the water cycle.

Rain

"Rain" is the name given to the droplets of water that fall from the sky. As water vapour rises from the earth and then cools in the troposphere, it condenses to create small droplets of water in clouds. These droplets combine, getting larger and heavier, and when they become too heavy to stay within the cloud, they fall to the ground.

Individual raindrops are often drawn or painted in the shape of a teardrop, but in real life rain never appears in this form. In fact, raindrops change shape as they fall through the sky.

1. Cloud droplets initially form as a ball, or "sphere", of water.

2. The balls of water bump into each other as they fall through the air, combining to create larger drops.

3. These larger raindrops fall to the ground more quickly. This increase in speed and airflow affects the raindrop's shape. It flattens out and bows at the bottom, creating a shape similar to a kidney bean or a hamburger bun.

4. The airflow continues to put pressure on the centre of the falling drop, causing the middle to thin out until the raindrop divides into two spherical droplets. The water droplets will then continue to change shape and divide until they reach a surface, the ground or a body of water.

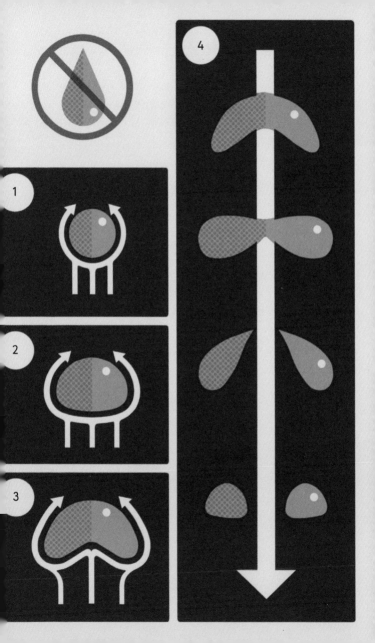

Extreme rainfall

When rain falls, water sometimes collects on the ground in small areas. These shallow pools are known as "puddles", and they often dry up, or "evaporate", or drain away into the soil as the weather brightens. But if rain falls for a longer period of time, if it is heavier rainfall than expected or if the drainage in the soil is poor, puddles can grow into ponds, pools or floods.

A flood occurs when an area of land that is usually dry is temporarily covered with water. One of the main natural causes of flooding is excessive rainfall. One of the most destructive types of flood is a "flash flood". These occur when heavy rain falls very quickly over an area of dry ground, causing a lot of damage. They appear without warning, and their impact on the local environment and people can be devastating.

Some parts of the world regularly experience intense weather events that create extremely wet conditions. These are known as "monsoons". The summer monsoon season of India and East Asia is famous for its heavy, or "torrential", rainfall between April and September. This rainfall feeds water supplies, helps to create electricity in hydroelectric power plants and helps crops to grow. However, it also causes severe flooding, deaths and environmental damage, such as mudslides.

Rainbows

When there is sunshine and rainfall at the same time, a multicoloured arc called a "rainbow" can appear in the sky. These mysterious and colourful arches have been given special meaning in many cultures and stories. To some, a rainbow is a bridge to other worlds. Others believe it to be the throne of a god or a signpost to a place where treasure can be found. But there is a scientific reason for the appearance of rainbows. A rainbow is created when rays of light hit droplets of water.

Natural light might appear to be white in colour, but it can be broken up into rays of light that appear as a mixture of different colours. As soon as sunlight enters a water droplet, it breaks up, or becomes "dispersed", into its different colours. Raindrops act like little mirrors, so as sunlight enters them, the light bounces off the back wall of the water droplet and is reflected back out again.

This reflection creates the colourful arc of a rainbow, as each colour leaves the raindrop at a slightly different angle. This is called "refraction". For example, the red light will leave the raindrop at a slightly wider angle than the orange light. This is how we get the colourful arc in the sky formed of red, orange, yellow, green, blue, indigo and violet.

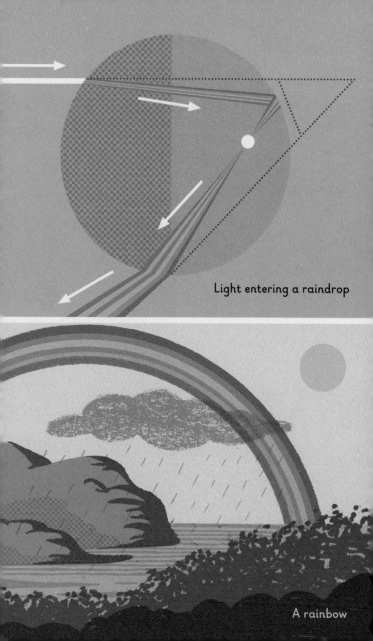

Light entering a raindrop

A rainbow

Clouds

Clouds exist where there is a change in air temperature. By looking at the clouds, we can see where the air becomes cold enough for water droplets to form into clouds.

- Below the clouds, the ground is being heated by the sun, and water molecules in bodies of water, such as lakes, puddles and ponds, start to evaporate. As the heated air rises, it carries the water vapour up into the atmosphere.

- The bottom of a cloud, or "cloud base", shows the exact point at which the atmosphere is cold enough for clouds to form. The rising water vapour will eventually reach a point in the atmosphere where the air temperature drops. This causes the water vapour to cool and condense back into liquid form. It then combines with other droplets to create floating masses called clouds.

- Inside the cloud, there can be currents of air moving up and down. This constant air change creates the cloud's fluffy top, which can be viewed from above.

Clouds appear as white masses in the sky because sunlight is white. When sunlight enters a cloud droplet, the light is scattered in different directions. Unlike the reflection and refraction that causes a rainbow, this scattering process doesn't split the light into colours but sends it in different directions. As clouds contain millions of water droplets, this large scattering of light makes the whole cloud appear white.

Cloud formations

The characteristics of a cloud are determined by how it is formed. Clouds form in different shapes and at different heights in the sky, and they have been given specific names to help meteorologists identify them. Here are a few examples:

- Wispy streamers of "cirrus" clouds form high up in the atmosphere and are made of ice crystals. They can be an indicator that windy or wet weather is on the way.

- Puffy "cumulus" clouds form when the air is rising in the atmosphere. Small cumulus clouds are sometimes called "fair weather clouds", forming on sunny days, but they can grow into towering "cumulonimbus" thunderclouds, which stretch all the way up to the top of the troposphere. Cumulonimbus clouds can bring heavy rain, hail, thunder, lightning and even tornadoes.

- Sheets of grey "stratus" cloud form when the air has cooled without rising. They can be created when the air is moving over colder ground or ocean, or when warm air meets cold air ahead of it. If stratus forms near the earth's surface, it is known as "fog" or, if it is less dense, "mist". Fog can cause visibility problems, especially for people driving on the road or flying.

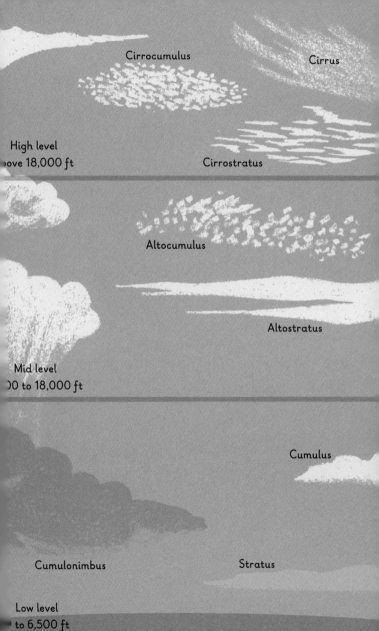

Cirrocumulus

Cirrus

Cirrostratus

High level
above 18,000 ft

Altocumulus

Altostratus

Mid level
6,500 to 18,000 ft

Cumulus

Cumulonimbus

Stratus

Low level
0 to 6,500 ft

Thunder and lightning

A storm is a general meteorological term used to describe a variety of strong weather events, from heavy rain and snow to strong winds and dark grey clouds.

A thunderstorm develops when the air in the atmosphere rises rapidly. When warm air rises quickly through the atmosphere, cloud droplets form an enormous, tower-shaped cumulonimbus cloud. Inside the cloud, currents of rising air move at wind speeds of up to 110 miles per hour (177 km/h) and carry frozen water droplets to heights where the air temperature is below freezing. Water vapour freezes in layers of ice on the rising frozen water droplets, creating hailstones.

The movement of rain and hail inside the cloud creates an electric charge, made up of positive and negative charges. As the positive charge rises to the top of the thundercloud, the negative charge sinks to the bottom. This causes tension as opposite charges are attracted to each other. When the attraction gets too strong, the charges come together very quickly in the cloud, or between the cloud and the ground. This movement creates the flash of light known as "lightning".

When a lightning bolt travels from the cloud to the ground, it heats the air to about 10,000°C (18,000°F). As the air heats up so quickly, it suddenly expands, causing a shock wave that creates a rumbling noise known as "thunder".

Wind

Wind is the movement of air. It is created by pressure differences in the atmosphere – the bigger the pressure difference, the faster the wind blows.

Wind is not something that can be seen, but we can feel its effect and its force. Wind rustles leaves on tree branches, creates patterns in sand dunes across deserts and causes the swells of ocean waves. It is a powerful force that humans have used to turn sails on windmills in order to grind flour and to power wind turbines to create electricity.

Wind can also be measured by watching the effect it has on other objects. The British naval commander Sir Francis Beaufort invented a wind force scale that can be used to estimate the speed of the wind using the conditions it creates on the earth's surface. The lowest unit of force on the Beaufort Wind Scale is Force 0, or "Calm", indicating a wind speed of less than 1 mile per hour (1.6 km/h), flat sea conditions and smoke rising vertically on the land. The highest unit is Force 12, or "Hurricane", indicating wind speeds of over 73 miles per hour (117 km/h), a sea completely white with spray and devastation on the land.

Tropical storms and tornadoes

Tropical storms form over warm ocean water in areas more than five degrees north or south of the equator – the invisible line around the centre of the earth. They are enormous circular storms that can be seen from space – with a clear "eye" (an area in the middle of the storm where calm weather is found), surrounded by an "eyewall" (a cloudy ring of violent thunderstorms). Tropical storms are often renamed depending on where in the world they form. Hurricanes, cyclones and typhoons are all types of tropical storm.

The damage a tropical storm can cause when it hits land depends on how fast and for how long its winds blow. Tropical storms that contain wind speeds of up to 190 miles per hour (306 km/h) can destroy homes, collapse walls and cause power shortages.

A tornado is a much smaller rotating wind storm, which forms when the rising air in a cumulonimbus cloud starts to spin. This creates a rotating funnel cloud at the base of the cumulonimbus, which, if it stretches down to the earth's surface, becomes a tornado.

Most tornadoes are 20 to 100 metres (66 to 328 ft) wide, with a travelling speed of 75 to 100 miles per hour (121 to 161 km/h). The low pressure at the centre of the tornado makes it act like a very powerful vacuum cleaner, capable of destroying buildings and uprooting trees.

Snow

Ice crystals, known as "snow", form when the air temperature falls below 2 degrees Celsius (36°F). Colder air means that as water vapour evaporates and condenses, ice crystals form inside the clouds instead of water droplets. Once an ice crystal has formed, the surrounding water vapour will then freeze on to it, or the crystal combines with other ice crystals to create a snowflake.

A snowflake will continue to combine and grow until it becomes too heavy for the cloud, which is when it falls as snow. If the surface temperature of the earth is at or below 2 degrees Celsius (36°F), snow will complete its journey to the ground in its frozen form. It will then stay there, or "settle", until air temperatures rise and cause the snow to melt into water.

If falling snow is met with warm air temperatures, it can partially melt. This creates a mixture of water droplets and ice crystals known as "sleet". Heavy bouts of sleet can create watery, puddle-like snow on the ground, which makes a slushing noise when it is walked through.

Snowfall can also turn into a snowstorm, or "blizzard", if it is met with strong, fast winds on its descent. Strong winds break ice crystals up into smaller fragments, so blizzards can sometimes create large, tightly packed banks of snow, or "snowdrifts", on the ground.

Snowflakes

Each snowflake is said to be unique. Although this is impossible to prove, the intricate and differing appearance of snowflakes when viewed under a microscope seems to support this belief.

The size and make-up of each snowflake depends on how many ice crystals group together to form a cluster. When snowflakes fall through dry, cool air, they reach the earth as small, powder-like flakes. Drier air contains less moisture, so the flakes don't collect any excess water as they fall. But when the temperature is slightly warmer, the edges of the snowflakes melt and this helps them to stick together, so bigger, heavier flakes are formed instead.

The first-known photographer of snowflakes was Wilson A. Bentley. He described snowflakes as "tiny miracles" and called snow crystals "ice flowers". In 1885, Bentley developed a method for taking photos of individual snowflakes through a microscope. This allowed him to capture the ice patterns on film before the snowflakes melted. The snowflakes on the opposite page are inspired by Bentley's photographs. Which one is your favourite?

A Ladybird Book

collectable books for curious kids

Animal Habitats

9780241416860

Baby Animals

9780241416907

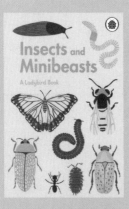

Insects and Minibeasts

9780241417034

Trees

9780241417218

SERIES 208

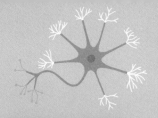

Electricity

9780241416945

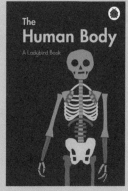

The Human Body

9780241416983

The Solar System

9780241417133

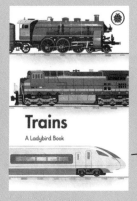

Trains

9780241417171

SERIES 218